MAD LIBS®

80s MAD LIBS

by Max Bisantz

MAD LIBS
An Imprint of Penguin Random House LLC, New York

Concept created by Roger Price & Leonard Stern

Cover illustration by Scott Brooks

Published by Mad Libs,
an imprint of Penguin Random House LLC, New York.
Printed in the USA.

Visit us online at www.penguinrandomhouse.com.

ISBN 9780593095553
5 7 9 10 8 6

MAD LIBS

INSTRUCTIONS

MAD LIBS® is a game for people who don't like games! It can be played by one, two, three, four, or forty.

• RIDICULOUSLY SIMPLE DIRECTIONS

In this tablet you will find stories containing blank spaces where words are left out. One player, the READER, selects one of these stories. The READER does not tell anyone what the story is about. Instead, he/she asks the other players, the WRITERS, to give him/her words. These words are used to fill in the blank spaces in the story.

• TO PLAY

The READER asks each WRITER in turn to call out a word—an adjective or a noun or whatever the space calls for—and uses them to fill in the blank spaces in the story. The result is a MAD LIBS® game.

When the READER then reads the completed MAD LIBS® game to the other players, they will discover that they have written a story that is fantastic, screamingly funny, shocking, silly, crazy, or just plain dumb—depending upon which words each WRITER called out.

• EXAMPLE (*Before* and *After*)

"_____!" he said _____
    EXCLAMATION   ADVERB

as he jumped into his convertible _____ and
                        NOUN

drove off with his _____ wife.
             ADJECTIVE

"**OUCH**!" he said **HAPPILY**
    EXCLAMATION   ADVERB

as he jumped into his convertible **CAT** and
                      NOUN

drove off with his **BRAVE** wife.
            ADJECTIVE

MAD LIBS

QUICK REVIEW

In case you have forgotten what adjectives, adverbs, nouns, and verbs are, here is a quick review:

An ADJECTIVE describes something or somebody. *Lumpy, soft, ugly, messy,* and *short* are adjectives.

An ADVERB tells how something is done. It modifies a verb and usually ends in "ly." *Modestly, stupidly, greedily,* and *carefully* are adverbs.

A NOUN is the name of a person, place, or thing. *Sidewalk, umbrella, bridle, bathtub,* and *nose* are nouns.

A VERB is an action word. *Run, pitch, jump,* and *swim* are verbs. Put the verbs in past tense if the directions say PAST TENSE. *Ran, pitched, jumped,* and *swam* are verbs in the past tense.

When we ask for A PLACE, we mean any sort of place: a country or city (*Spain, Cleveland*) or a room (*bathroom, kitchen*).

An EXCLAMATION or SILLY WORD is any sort of funny sound, gasp, grunt, or outcry, like *Wow!, Ouch!, Whomp!, Ick!,* and *Gadzooks!*

When we ask for specific words, like a NUMBER, a COLOR, an ANIMAL, or a PART OF THE BODY, we mean a word that is one of those things, like *seven, blue, horse,* or *head.*

When we ask for a PLURAL, it means more than one. For example, *cat* pluralized is *cats.*

MAD LIBS® is fun to play with friends, but you can also play it by yourself! To begin with, DO NOT look at the story on the page below. Fill in the blanks on this page with the words called for. Then, using the words you have selected, fill in the blank spaces in the story.

Now you've created your own hilarious MAD LIBS® game!

BACK TO THE 80s

VERB _____

COLOR _____

VERB (PAST TENSE) _____

NOUN _____

PLURAL NOUN _____

VERB _____

ADJECTIVE _____

VERB ENDING IN "ING" _____

TYPE OF CLOTHING _____

TYPE OF CLOTHING (PLURAL) _____

VERB (PAST TENSE) _____

VERB _____

NOUN _____

PART OF THE BODY _____

VERB _____

EXCLAMATION _____

VERB _____

ADJECTIVE _____

MAD LIBS®

BACK TO THE 80s

Quick! Grab the plutonium and _____ inside this DeLorean.
                                      VERB

My name is Dr. _____ , and I _____ here
                    COLOR   VERB (PAST TENSE)

from the future. We're taking a/an _____ back in time to the
                                          NOUN

1980s, a decade all about big hair and even bigger _____ .
                                                        PLURAL NOUN

_____ yourself in—this is going to be a/an _____
      VERB   ADJECTIVE

ride. First, we'll stop at a suburban _____ mall to buy
                                        VERB ENDING IN "ING"

you some new clothes, like a neon _____ and
                                        TYPE OF CLOTHING

acid-washed _____ . That way, no one will know
              TYPE OF CLOTHING (PLURAL)

that you _____ from the future! Next, we'll head to
              VERB (PAST TENSE)

the arcade to _____ some video games. But watch out!
                    VERB

Danger lurks around every _____ . You might find yourself
                                NOUN

face-to- _____ with a stranger, or worse—a yuppy!
              PART OF THE BODY

Whatever you _____ , you must remember to "Just Say
                    VERB

_____ ." So sit back, relax, and try not to _____ into
  EXCLAMATION   VERB

your parents. That can get pretty _____ , pretty fast.
                                        ADJECTIVE

MAD LIBS® is fun to play with friends, but you can also play it by yourself! To begin with, DO NOT look at the story on the page below. Fill in the blanks on this page with the words called for. Then, using the words you have selected, fill in the blank spaces in the story.

Now you've created your own hilarious MAD LIBS® game!

BETA TO THE MAX

PERSON IN ROOM _____

SILLY WORD _____

PLURAL NOUN _____

VERB _____

NUMBER _____

NOUN _____

NOUN _____

PERSON IN ROOM _____

VEHICLE _____

NOUN _____

NUMBER _____

VERB ENDING IN "ING" _____

NUMBER _____

TYPE OF FOOD _____

NOUN _____

VERB _____

NUMBER _____

MAD LIBS®

BETA TO THE MAX

Come on down to _____'s Discount Electronics this
                                 PERSON IN ROOM

Sunday for the best deals this side of the _____ River! We
                                              SILLY WORD

have fax _____. We have Betamax. If you want it, we
              PLURAL NOUN

_____ it. Check out this state-of-the-art VCR for only
        VERB

_____ bucks. Watch movies from the comfort of your very own
   NUMBER

_____! And take a look at this answering _____
   NOUN   NOUN

for your phone. You'll never miss a message from dear old Aunt

_____ again. And speaking of phones, why not put one
  PERSON IN ROOM

in your car, or your van, or your _____? Better yet, take
                                      VEHICLE

your phone on the go with a cellular _____—now
                                           NOUN

_____ percent off! But that's not all. This Sunday only, we're
   NUMBER

_____ home computers for half price. Weighing in
  VERB ENDING IN "ING"

at only fifty-seven pounds, _____ ounces, this lightweight
                             NUMBER

machine makes your parents' abacus look like chopped _____.
                                                 TYPE OF FOOD

Don't miss this once-in-a/an- _____ opportunity to invest in
                             NOUN

your future. So _____ your calendars for this Sunday.
                 VERB

Lucky customer number _____ receives a free beeper!
                      NUMBER

MAD LIBS® is fun to play with friends, but you can also play it by yourself! To begin with, DO NOT look at the story on the page below. Fill in the blanks on this page with the words called for. Then, using the words you have selected, fill in the blank spaces in the story.

Now you've created your own hilarious MAD LIBS® game!

SHOP TILL YOU DROP

ADJECTIVE _____

VERB _____

VERB ENDING IN "ING" _____

PART OF THE BODY (PLURAL) _____

NUMBER _____

ADJECTIVE _____

PART OF THE BODY _____

ADJECTIVE _____

ARTICLE OF CLOTHING (PLURAL) _____

COLOR _____

NOUN _____

NOUN _____

VERB ENDING IN "S" _____

NOUN _____

VEHICLE _____

NOUN _____

ARTICLE OF CLOTHING (PLURAL) _____

MAD LIBS®

SHOP TILL YOU DROP

Debbie: We need to look _____ for the first day of school,
                              ADJECTIVE

Tiffany. What should we _____ at the _____
                              VERB   VERB ENDING IN "ING"

mall?

Tiffany: I need to get my _____ on some denim.
                              PART OF THE BODY (PLURAL)

Let's buy _____-dollar jeans and then rip them up. All the
                    NUMBER

_____ kids are doing it.
     ADJECTIVE

Debbie: We should also buy fuzzy _____ warmers.
                                        PART OF THE BODY

My knees get _____ in the winter. Let's grab neon
                    ADJECTIVE

_____, too. I want my clothes to match my
ARTICLE OF CLOTHING (PLURAL)

personality: bright _____! It's like Cyndi says: "Girls just
                         COLOR

want to have _____."
                  NOUN

Tiffany: We have to buy scrunchies and hair _____, too.
                                                    NOUN

I'm gonna tease my hair until it _____ for forgiveness.
                                  VERB ENDING IN "S"

Debbie: Tiffany, you are funnier than Andrew Dice _____!
                                                         NOUN

Let's hop in your dad's _____ and use his credit
                            VEHICLE

_____. I don't want to miss the sale on Members Only
     NOUN

_____.
ARTICLE OF CLOTHING (PLURAL)

MAD LIBS® is fun to play with friends, but you can also play it by yourself! To begin with, DO NOT look at the story on the page below. Fill in the blanks on this page with the words called for. Then, using the words you have selected, fill in the blank spaces in the story.

Now you've created your own hilarious MAD LIBS® game!

I WANT MY MTV!

PERSON IN ROOM _____

PLURAL NOUN _____

VERB ENDING IN "ING" _____

OCCUPATION (PLURAL) _____

VERB ENDING IN "ING" _____

VERB _____

NOUN _____

PART OF THE BODY (PLURAL) _____

ADJECTIVE _____

OCCUPATION (PLURAL) _____

NOUN _____

PLURAL NOUN _____

COLOR _____

NOUN _____

NOUN _____

PART OF THE BODY _____

MAD LIBS®

I WANT MY MTV!

Yo! It's your favorite VJ, _____ , coming to you live from
                        PERSON IN ROOM

MTV's first ever Video Music _____ . We are witnessing
                            PLURAL NOUN

history in the _____ right now as the hottest
              VERB ENDING IN "ING"

_____ in the world come together for one night only.
OCCUPATION (PLURAL)

We've got the _____ Heads rapping with
             VERB ENDING IN "ING"

_____ -DMC. We've got disco diva Donna _____
     VERB   NOUN

pulling ZZ Top's _____ . And let's not forget these
                PART OF THE BODY (PLURAL)

_____ performances coming up. The _____ are
   ADJECTIVE   OCCUPATION (PLURAL)

going to perform their big hit "Every _____ You Take."
                                      NOUN

And do I hear wedding _____ in Madonna's future? She's
                     PLURAL NOUN

wearing a/an _____ bridal gown to perform her hit song
            COLOR

"Like a/an _____ ." So whether you like rap, metal, or
          NOUN

_____ , stay tuned. When it comes to music, MTV has got
   NOUN

your _____ .
    PART OF THE BODY

MAD LIBS® is fun to play with friends, but you can also play it by yourself! To begin with, DO NOT look at the story on the page below. Fill in the blanks on this page with the words called for. Then, using the words you have selected, fill in the blank spaces in the story.

Now you've created your own hilarious MAD LIBS® game!

CHAMPAGNE AND SHOULDER PADS

ANIMAL _____

FIRST NAME _____

VERB ENDING IN "ING" _____

NOUN _____

PERSON IN ROOM _____

NOUN _____

PART OF THE BODY _____

PERSON IN ROOM _____

TYPE OF FOOD _____

VERB ENDING IN "ING" _____

NOUN _____

ARTICLE OF CLOTHING _____

FIRST NAME _____

COUNTRY _____

VERB _____

VERB (PAST TENSE) _____

Previously on _____ *Crest*, oil tycoon _____
                    ANIMAL   FIRST NAME

disowns his family by _____ his BMW into a/an
                        VERB ENDING IN "ING"

_____ . Meanwhile, ex-wife _____ fires a loaded
      NOUN   PERSON IN ROOM

_____ at a horse show, causing real estate mogul Bobby to
      NOUN

get kicked in the _____ . This, of course, is payback for
                    PART OF THE BODY

_____ poisoning the champagne and _____
      PERSON IN ROOM   TYPE OF FOOD

luncheon for Lance, who gets locked in a remote sanatorium for

_____ the senator's illegitimate _____ . The
   VERB ENDING IN "ING"   NOUN

episode ends with Krystle using her pearl _____ to
                                            ARTICLE OF CLOTHING

choke _____ for her blackmail scheme. In this episode,
        FIRST NAME

will Amanda fall for the charms of Prince Michael of _____ ?
                                                        COUNTRY

Does Monica finally _____ for divorce? And for goodness
                        VERB

sake, will we ever learn "Who _____ J.R.?"
                                VERB (PAST TENSE)

MAD LIBS® is fun to play with friends, but you can also play it by yourself! To begin with, DO NOT look at the story on the page below. Fill in the blanks on this page with the words called for. Then, using the words you have selected, fill in the blank spaces in the story.

Now you've created your own hilarious MAD LIBS® game!

RING OF CHAMPIONS

PLURAL NOUN _____

NUMBER _____

ADJECTIVE _____

NOUN _____

NOUN _____

PERSON IN ROOM _____

NUMBER _____

NOUN _____

VERB ENDING IN "ING" _____

PLURAL NOUN _____

FIRST NAME _____

NOUN _____

ADJECTIVE _____

NOUN _____

VERB _____

MAD LIBS®

RING OF CHAMPIONS

Welcome to the Opening Ceremony of the 1988 Summer Olympic

_____. As we wait for _____ athletes to enter
<u>PLURAL NOUN</u>   <u>NUMBER</u>

Olympic Stadium, let's look back on some of the most _____
                                                          <u>ADJECTIVE</u>

moments from this decade's Games:

- We'll never forget 1980's "Miracle on _____," when the
                                              <u>NOUN</u>

  US men's hockey team defeated the Soviet team and went on to

  win the gold _____. At the Summer Games, gymnast
                    <u>NOUN</u>

  _____ Comăneci won _____ gold medals for
  <u>PERSON IN ROOM</u>   <u>NUMBER</u>

  her spectacular work on the balance _____.
                                            <u>NOUN</u>

- 1984 welcomed new sports—synchronized _____
                                               <u>VERB ENDING IN "ING"</u>

  and rhythmic _____—to the Games.
                              <u>PLURAL NOUN</u>

  _____ Lewis smashed records by winning big in the
  <u>FIRST NAME</u>

  track-and- _____ events.
                  <u>NOUN</u>

- Who can forget the _____ bobsled team from
                            <u>ADJECTIVE</u>

  sunny Jamaica at the 1988 Winter Games? They crashed their

  _____, but won the hearts of the world!
  <u>NOUN</u>

Now, let's turn back to the live event and let the Games _____!
                                                              <u>VERB</u>

MAD LIBS® is fun to play with friends, but you can also play it by yourself! To begin with, DO NOT look at the story on the page below. Fill in the blanks on this page with the words called for. Then, using the words you have selected, fill in the blank spaces in the story.

Now you've created your own hilarious MAD LIBS® game!

HIT RECORD

VERB _____

NOUN _____

NOUN _____

VERB ENDING IN "ING" _____

COLOR _____

VERB _____

OCCUPATION (PLURAL) _____

FIRST NAME _____

NOUN _____

VERB _____

VERB _____

NOUN _____

ADJECTIVE _____

ARTICLE OF CLOTHING (PLURAL) _____

NOUN _____

NOUN _____

PERSON IN ROOM _____

MAD LIBS

HIT RECORD

With my new camcorder, I'm going to _____ the
VERB

most amazing films in the world! I'll sell more tickets than

_____-busters and *Raiders of the Lost* _____
NOUN   NOUN

combined. First, I'll write a script that's like _____
VERB ENDING IN "ING"

to America mixed with _____ *Velvet.* I love comedies that also
COLOR

make you _____. I'll cast the most famous _____
VERB   OCCUPATION (PLURAL)

in Hollywood, like _____ Cruise and Whoopi
FIRST NAME

_____-berg. Then it's lights, camera, _____! My
NOUN   VERB

movie will have more chase scenes than _____ *Hard* and more
VERB

explosions than *Lethal* _____. I'll add some cool narrators
NOUN

like in *Do the* _____ *Thing*, and then I'll scare the
ADJECTIVE

_____ off the audience like *A Nightmare on*
ARTICLE OF CLOTHING (PLURAL)

_____ *Street.* When I accept my Academy _____ for
NOUN   NOUN

Best Director, I'll thank Grandma _____ for buying me
PERSON IN ROOM

this VHS camcorder!

MAD LIBS® is fun to play with friends, but you can also play it by yourself! To begin with, DO NOT look at the story on the page below. Fill in the blanks on this page with the words called for. Then, using the words you have selected, fill in the blank spaces in the story.

Now you've created your own hilarious MAD LIBS® game!

GIMME A BEAT

VERB _____

OCCUPATION _____

ADJECTIVE _____

CELEBRITY _____

PART OF THE BODY (PLURAL) _____

NOUN _____

VERB _____

PLURAL NOUN _____

ADJECTIVE _____

ADJECTIVE _____

NOUN _____

NUMBER _____

NOUN _____

ADVERB _____

OCCUPATION _____

PLURAL NOUN _____

VERB ENDING IN "ING" _____

MAD LIBS

GIMME A BEAT

Some people say you can't _____ a broken heart. Those
                                 VERB

people never met _____ Robert Jarvik, creator of the world's
                    OCCUPATION

first _____ heart. _____ started building artificial
      ADJECTIVE   CELEBRITY

_____ when he was a student at the University of
PART OF THE BODY (PLURAL)

Utah School of _____ . But he wanted to _____
                   NOUN   VERB

a replacement heart that could save people's _____ . Most
                                               PLURAL NOUN

people thought this was a/an _____ idea. The heart is one
                               ADJECTIVE

of the most _____ organs in the human _____ .
              ADJECTIVE   NOUN

But Jarvik tested _____ different models made from plastic,
                     NUMBER

polyurethane, and _____ until he knew his heart was safe.
                     NOUN

In 1982, a surgeon _____ implanted Dr. Jarvik's artificial
                      ADVERB

heart into a brave _____ who volunteered for surgery.
                      OCCUPATION

Since then, thousands of _____ have been saved
                            PLURAL NOUN

by artificial hearts. Thanks to Robert Jarvik, artificial hearts keep

_____ in chests around the world.
VERB ENDING IN "ING"

MAD LIBS® is fun to play with friends, but you can also play it by yourself! To begin with, DO NOT look at the story on the page below. Fill in the blanks on this page with the words called for. Then, using the words you have selected, fill in the blank spaces in the story.

Now you've created your own hilarious MAD LIBS® game!

JELLY BEANS IN THE WHITE HOUSE

NOUN _____

NOUN _____

ADVERB _____

NOUN _____

VERB _____

NUMBER _____

NOUN _____

NOUN _____

OCCUPATION _____

PLURAL NOUN _____

NOUN _____

VERB _____

PLURAL NOUN _____

VERB _____

NOUN _____

ANIMAL _____

PLURAL NOUN _____

VERB _____

MAD LIBS
JELLY BEANS IN
THE WHITE HOUSE

By 1940, Ronald Reagan was a big Hollywood movie _____.
                                                        NOUN

He starred in his film debut *Love Is on the* _____ and dazzled
                                                   NOUN

in the movie *Knute Rockne—* _____ *American*, playing
                                    ADVERB

a/an _____ named "the Gipper." The nickname would
           NOUN

_____ with him for the rest of his life. Reagan served in World
    VERB

War _____ stationed in _____ City, California. By
        NUMBER   NOUN

1947, he was president of the Screen Actors _____, and by
                                                   NOUN

1967, he was elected _____ of California. Reagan was elected
                          OCCUPATION

president of the United _____ of America in 1980 with
                             PLURAL NOUN

George H. W. _____ as vice president. He transformed the
                  NOUN

economy with _____-down economics. Meanwhile, the
                     VERB

First Lady fought against _____ with her "Just _____
                              PLURAL NOUN   VERB

No" campaign. In 1981, Reagan survived a brutal _____
                                                        NOUN

attempt, and in 1984, he was reelected. After his presidency, Reagan

spent time at his _____ ranch in California. Historians
                       ANIMAL

note that Reagan started eating jelly _____ to help him
                                            PLURAL NOUN

_____ smoking.
    VERB

MAD LIBS® is fun to play with friends, but you can also play it by yourself! To begin with, DO NOT look at the story on the page below. Fill in the blanks on this page with the words called for. Then, using the words you have selected, fill in the blank spaces in the story.

Now you've created your own hilarious MAD LIBS® game!

CARTOON LINEUP

PLURAL NOUN _____

NUMBER _____

PLURAL NOUN _____

NOUN _____

ADJECTIVE _____

ANIMAL (PLURAL) _____

NOUN _____

VERB _____

NOUN _____

VERB _____

VERB _____

FIRST NAME _____

NOUN _____

VERB _____

VERB ENDING IN "ING" _____

ANIMAL _____

MAD LIBS

CARTOON LINEUP

Sister: Give me the remote, I want to watch *Jem and the*

_____ .
   PLURAL NOUN

Brother: I'm _____ days older than you, so I get to choose.
       NUMBER

We're going to watch *He-Man and the* _____ *of the Universe*!
                        PLURAL NOUN

Sister: Ick! *She-Ra: Princess of* _____ is way more
                             NOUN

_____ than *He-Man*. Why don't we just turn on
    ADJECTIVE

Thunder- _____ ?
      ANIMAL (PLURAL)

Brother: Because you flushed my Lion-O action figure down the

_____ and now I don't like that show. _____ me the
  NOUN   VERB

remote! I have to find out if Skeletor conquered the fortress at Castle

Gray- _____ .
     NOUN

Sister: He's never going to _____ the fortress! If I don't get to
                          VERB

_____ *Jem*, how about we both watch *G.I.* _____ ?
  VERB   FIRST NAME

Brother: How about I transform into Optimus _____ and
                                   NOUN

_____ you instead?
  VERB

Sister: I'm _____ Mom you said that, and then I'm
         VERB ENDING IN "ING"

going to watch *My Little* _____ just because you hate it!
                 ANIMAL

MAD LIBS® is fun to play with friends, but you can also play it by yourself! To begin with, DO NOT look at the story on the page below. Fill in the blanks on this page with the words called for. Then, using the words you have selected, fill in the blank spaces in the story.

Now you've created your own hilarious MAD LIBS® game!

FEEL THE BURN

PERSON IN ROOM _____

NOUN _____

OCCUPATION _____

PART OF THE BODY _____

FIRST NAME _____

PLURAL NOUN _____

ADJECTIVE _____

ARTICLE OF CLOTHING (PLURAL) _____

PART OF THE BODY (PLURAL) _____

VERB ENDING IN "ING" _____

ADJECTIVE _____

PLURAL NOUN _____

NUMBER _____

TYPE OF LIQUID _____

ADJECTIVE _____

VERB (PAST TENSE) _____

NOUN _____

My name is _____, and power aerobics saved my
                    PERSON IN ROOM

_____. I was an out-of-shape _____ who barely
         NOUN   OCCUPATION

lifted her _____ off the couch all day. Then, I bought
            PART OF THE BODY

_____ Fonda's workout video, and it suddenly hit me like
     FIRST NAME

a sack of _____. In order to be happy and _____,
           PLURAL NOUN   ADJECTIVE

I need to wear spandex _____ and stretch my
                        ARTICLE OF CLOTHING (PLURAL)

arms and _____ every day. From there, I started
          PART OF THE BODY (PLURAL)

_____ aerobics classes at the local gym to learn all the
VERB ENDING IN "ING"

steps: high kicks, _____ lunges, and fancy _____.
                    ADJECTIVE   PLURAL NOUN

I lost over _____ pounds in blood, sweat, and _____
              NUMBER   TYPE OF LIQUID

by power squatting and _____ jumping. I got my chance at
                         ADJECTIVE

the big leagues when I _____ in the National Aerobic
                         VERB (PAST TENSE)

Championship in 1987. I didn't win a gold _____, but I won
                                            NOUN

a new lease on life.

MAD LIBS® is fun to play with friends, but you can also play it by yourself! To begin with, DO NOT look at the story on the page below. Fill in the blanks on this page with the words called for. Then, using the words you have selected, fill in the blank spaces in the story.

Now you've created your own hilarious MAD LIBS® game!

A 1980s CHRISTMAS WISH LIST

ADJECTIVE _____

NUMBER _____

LETTER OF THE ALPHABET _____

PLURAL NOUN _____

TYPE OF FOOD _____

ADJECTIVE _____

VERB _____

ADJECTIVE _____

VERB _____

NOUN _____

FIRST NAME _____

ANIMAL _____

NOUN _____

ANIMAL (PLURAL) _____

COLOR _____

NUMBER _____

TYPE OF FOOD (PLURAL) _____

ADJECTIVE _____

MAD LIBS
A 1980s CHRISTMAS
WISH LIST

Dear Santa,

I've been a/an _____ child this year and only got grounded
ADJECTIVE

_____ times. I even got a/an _____ on my math
NUMBER   LETTER OF THE ALPHABET

test! With that in mind, I have a long list of _____ I want
PLURAL NOUN

this holiday season:

- A/An _____ Patch Doll. These _____ pals are all
  TYPE OF FOOD   ADJECTIVE

  the rage, and if I don't get one, I'm going to _____ .
  VERB

- Rainbow _____ . I _____ the TV show every
  ADJECTIVE   VERB

  week, and I wish I had a beauty _____ just like she does!
  NOUN

- _____ Ruxpin, the stuffed _____ that reads.
  FIRST NAME   ANIMAL

  He could read me a bedtime _____ every night.
  NOUN

- Pound _____ . I want _____ ones with spots.
  ANIMAL (PLURAL)   COLOR

Santa, I promise to leave you _____ cookies and
NUMBER

_____ for your reindeer . . . if you leave me feeling
TYPE OF FOOD (PLURAL)

_____ on Christmas morning!
ADJECTIVE

MAD LIBS® is fun to play with friends, but you can also play it by yourself! To begin with, DO NOT look at the story on the page below. Fill in the blanks on this page with the words called for. Then, using the words you have selected, fill in the blank spaces in the story.

Now you've created your own hilarious MAD LIBS® game!

LET'S WRESTLE

NOUN _____

PART OF THE BODY _____

PLURAL NOUN _____

NUMBER _____

VERB ENDING IN "ING" _____

NOUN _____

LETTER OF THE ALPHABET _____

PART OF THE BODY _____

NOUN _____

PART OF THE BODY _____

PLURAL NOUN _____

ANIMAL _____

NOUN _____

ADJECTIVE _____

COUNTRY _____

NUMBER _____

ARTICLE OF CLOTHING _____

MAD LIBS

LET'S WRESTLE

I've just returned from WrestleMania, hosted by the World Wrestling

_____ , and my _____ is blown. You wouldn't
　　　NOUN　　　　　　　　　　　PART OF THE BODY

believe the massive _____ I saw throwing down in the ring.
　　　　　　　　　　　　PLURAL NOUN

The arena was packed with _____ fans who were all cheering
　　　　　　　　　　　　　　　　NUMBER

and _____ . I watched _____ Hogan and
　　　VERB ENDING IN "ING"　　　　　　　　　　NOUN

Mr. _____ go head-to-_____ with
　　　LETTER OF THE ALPHABET　　　　　　　　PART OF THE BODY

a duo of bad guys. They smashed a/an _____ over one
　　　　　　　　　　　　　　　　　　　　　NOUN

guy's _____ ! After the show, the wrestlers signed
　　　PART OF THE BODY

_____ for all their fans. I got to meet my favorite wrestlers,
　　PLURAL NOUN

Junkyard _____ and Andre the _____ . I heard
　　　　　　　ANIMAL　　　　　　　　　　　　　NOUN

WrestleMania was so _____ , they're going to do another one
　　　　　　　　　　　ADJECTIVE

in _____ ! I would travel _____ miles to see these athletes
　　COUNTRY　　　　　　　　　　　NUMBER

in the ring again. Thankfully, I bought an official _____
　　　　　　　　　　　　　　　　　　　　　　ARTICLE OF CLOTHING

to remember this day forever!

MAD LIBS® is fun to play with friends, but you can also play it by yourself! To begin with, DO NOT look at the story on the page below. Fill in the blanks on this page with the words called for. Then, using the words you have selected, fill in the blank spaces in the story.

Now you've created your own hilarious MAD LIBS® game!

HOLDING HANDS

PART OF THE BODY (PLURAL) _____

ADJECTIVE _____

VERB _____

ADJECTIVE _____

ANIMAL _____

PLURAL NOUN _____

ADJECTIVE _____

OCCUPATION (PLURAL) _____

NOUN _____

ADJECTIVE _____

VERB _____

VERB _____

ADJECTIVE _____

NOUN _____

COUNTRY _____

VERB _____

MAD LIBS®

HOLDING HANDS

Taylor: Can you believe that _____ Across America
<u>PART OF THE BODY (PLURAL)</u>
is this Sunday? It's gonna be the most _____ event to ever
<u>ADJECTIVE</u>
happen. People across the country will _____ hands to form
<u>VERB</u>
a human chain from sea to _____ sea. They say even Mickey
<u>ADJECTIVE</u>
_____ is going to join! It's supposed to represent hope and
<u>ANIMAL</u>
_____ .
<u>PLURAL NOUN</u>

Ren: Sounds even more_____ than last year when all those
<u>ADJECTIVE</u>
celebrity _____ sang "We Are the _____ ."
<u>OCCUPATION (PLURAL)</u>   <u>NOUN</u>

Taylor: That was nothing compared to this _____ moment in
<u>ADJECTIVE</u>
history.

Ren: Well, I'm not going to _____ hands with a stranger. I
<u>VERB</u>
don't want to _____ any cooties.
<u>VERB</u>

Taylor: Don't be such a/an _____ sport. How can we make
<u>ADJECTIVE</u>
the world a better _____ if we don't take risks? I'm going to
<u>NOUN</u>
Hands Across _____ , and there's nothing you can
<u>COUNTRY</u>
_____ to stop me!
<u>VERB</u>

MAD LIBS® is fun to play with friends, but you can also play it by yourself! To begin with, DO NOT look at the story on the page below. Fill in the blanks on this page with the words called for. Then, using the words you have selected, fill in the blank spaces in the story.

Now you've created your own hilarious MAD LIBS® game!

PUMP UP THE JAM

ADJECTIVE _____

VERB _____

ADJECTIVE _____

PART OF THE BODY _____

NOUN _____

ADJECTIVE _____

ANIMAL _____

NOUN _____

VERB _____

NOUN _____

VERB _____

VERB _____

ARTICLE OF CLOTHING (PLURAL) _____

EXCLAMATION _____

NOUN _____

MAD LIBS®

PUMP UP THE JAM

It's a/an _____ time to be a music lover now that you can
      ADJECTIVE

_____ your favorite songs on the go! Are you a/an
    VERB

_____ Walkman listener, or an over-the-_____
  ADJECTIVE   PART OF THE BODY

boom box blaster? Take this _____ to find out!
                           NOUN

- Are your arms really _____?
                  ADJECTIVE

- Do you strut down the street, proud as a/an _____?
                                  ANIMAL

- Are you always the last to leave a/an _____?
                           NOUN

- Are you always first to _____ at karaoke?
                    VERB

- Do you think the whole wide _____ should
                           NOUN

  _____ to your music?
    VERB

- Do you think you _____ the sidewalk or something?
                VERB

- Do you have the nerve to wear _____ after
                      ARTICLE OF CLOTHING (PLURAL)

April?

If you answered "_____" to most of these questions,
               EXCLAMATION

you should buy a/an _____!
            NOUN

MAD LIBS® is fun to play with friends, but you can also play it by yourself! To begin with, DO NOT look at the story on the page below. Fill in the blanks on this page with the words called for. Then, using the words you have selected, fill in the blank spaces in the story.

Now you've created your own hilarious MAD LIBS® game!

MIDNIGHT ARCADE

PLURAL NOUN _____

ADJECTIVE _____

NUMBER _____

FIRST NAME _____

TYPE OF FOOD _____

VERB ENDING IN "ING" _____

ADJECTIVE _____

ANIMAL _____

PART OF THE BODY (PLURAL) _____

NOUN _____

FIRST NAME _____

NOUN _____

NOUN _____

LETTER OF THE ALPHABET _____

PART OF THE BODY _____

ADJECTIVE _____

VERB _____

MAD LIBS

MIDNIGHT ARCADE

Pac-Dude: Now that all the _____ are gone for the day,
PLURAL NOUN

let's get one thing straight. This arcade isn't big enough for all these

_____ fancy characters.
ADJECTIVE

Paperkid: You said it. Back in my day, you only needed _____
NUMBER

pixels to have a good time.

Pac-Dude: Have you seen this new plumber named _____?
FIRST NAME

He and Princess _____ hang out in the sewers all day
TYPE OF FOOD

_____ mushrooms. That can't be _____ for kids.
VERB ENDING IN "ING"   ADJECTIVE

Paperkid: And don't get me started with _____ Kong. He'll
ANIMAL

smash anything he gets his fuzzy _____ on. I saw
PART OF THE BODY (PLURAL)

him smash Frogger as he was trying to cross the _____!
NOUN

Pac-Dude: What about _____ in *The* _____ *of*
FIRST NAME   NOUN

Zelda? He needs to watch where he swings that _____.
NOUN

One time he almost smacked _____ *bert in the
LETTER OF THE ALPHABET

_____.
PART OF THE BODY

Paperkid: Things aren't like when we were _____. Now
ADJECTIVE

people can _____ games in their own homes!
VERB

MAD LIBS® is fun to play with friends, but you can also play it by yourself! To begin with, DO NOT look at the story on the page below. Fill in the blanks on this page with the words called for. Then, using the words you have selected, fill in the blank spaces in the story.

Now you've created your own hilarious MAD LIBS® game!

BROADWAY COMES TO A CRASH

VERB _____

ADVERB _____

NUMBER _____

ADJECTIVE _____

VERB _____

VERB ENDING IN "ING" _____

NOUN _____

PART OF THE BODY _____

PLURAL NOUN _____

A PLACE _____

VERB _____

PERSON IN ROOM _____

COLOR _____

PLURAL NOUN _____

VERB (PAST TENSE) _____

ANIMAL (PLURAL) _____

MAD LIBS
BROADWAY
COMES TO A CRASH

When people in the theater tell you to " _____ a leg," they
                                          VERB
don't mean it _____ ! I've been in _____ Broadway
                  ADVERB   NUMBER
shows, and I always keep myself healthy and _____ . But after
                                                ADJECTIVE
last night, I will never _____ on a Broadway stage again! There
                              VERB
I was, _____ across the boards in *The Phantom of the*
        VERB ENDING IN "ING"
_____ , when a chandelier came crashing down right on my
    NOUN
_____ ! It hurt so bad, I swear I could see _____ .
 PART OF THE BODY   PLURAL NOUN
The stage manager rushed me to (the) _____ , but it was
                                          A PLACE
too late. I will never dance or _____ again! I starred in
                                      VERB
Sunday in the Park with _____ . I understudied for Effie
                            PERSON IN ROOM
_____ in *Dream-_____* ! Oh well. The curtain
    COLOR   PLURAL NOUN
may have _____ on my career, but I'll always have
           VERB (PAST TENSE)
my "Memory." After all, that was the name of my hit song from the
musical _____ .
         ANIMAL (PLURAL)

MAD LIBS® is fun to play with friends, but you can also play it by yourself! To begin with, DO NOT look at the story on the page below. Fill in the blanks on this page with the words called for. Then, using the words you have selected, fill in the blank spaces in the story.

Now you've created your own hilarious MAD LIBS® game!

A ROYAL WEDDING

NOUN _____

PART OF THE BODY (PLURAL) _____

PERSON IN ROOM _____

OCCUPATION _____

COLOR _____

NOUN _____

NUMBER _____

NOUN _____

NOUN _____

VERB _____

ADJECTIVE _____

TYPE OF BUILDING _____

PLURAL NOUN _____

NOUN _____

ANIMAL (PLURAL) _____

NOUN _____

MAD LIBS

A ROYAL WEDDING

The look of _____ was in Prince Charles's
                        NOUN

_____ when he wed Diana at St. _____'s
PART OF THE BODY (PLURAL)   PERSON IN ROOM

Cathedral earlier this morning. The future _____ of
                                              OCCUPATION

England looked dapper as can be in his _____
                                              COLOR

naval commander's uniform . . . but it was shy Di who stole the

_____. Wearing a dress made from _____ meters of
     NOUN   NUMBER

ivory _____, she floated down the aisle like a cloud in the
        NOUN

_____. "With this ring, I thee _____,"
     NOUN   VERB

said the dashing prince to his _____ princess. From
                                   ADJECTIVE

there, the couple raced off to Buckingham _____
                                            TYPE OF BUILDING

for breakfast with _____—but not before sneaking a quick
                    PLURAL NOUN

_____ on the balcony for all to see! What a cheeky move from
   NOUN

these two love-_____. Folks across the Commonwealth
                ANIMAL (PLURAL)

are already calling this event "the _____ of the century"!
                                        NOUN

MAD LIBS® is fun to play with friends, but you can also play it by yourself! To begin with, DO NOT look at the story on the page below. Fill in the blanks on this page with the words called for. Then, using the words you have selected, fill in the blank spaces in the story.

Now you've created your own hilarious MAD LIBS® game!

RAP HISTORY RAP

VERB _____

ADJECTIVE _____

VERB ENDING IN "ING" _____

LETTER OF THE ALPHABET _____

VERB ENDING IN "ING" _____

NOUN _____

NOUN _____

NOUN _____

ADJECTIVE _____

TYPE OF FOOD _____

ADJECTIVE _____

ARTICLE OF CLOTHING _____

NUMBER _____

VERB _____

NOUN _____

VERB _____

COUNTRY _____

It's _____ -DMC, the _____ three,

VERB   ADJECTIVE

goin' on a trip back in rap history.

You got Run and DMC _____ up on the scene,

VERB ENDING IN "ING"

with Jam Master _____ _____ beats

LETTER OF THE ALPHABET   VERB ENDING IN "ING"

loud and clean.

Public _____ came next, so let's pay respect.

NOUN

Flavor Flav wore a giant _____ around his neck.

NOUN

Then step your _____ up, if you're a/an _____ stepper,

NOUN   ADJECTIVE

and listen to the hits from _____-N-Pepa.

TYPE OF FOOD

We got LL _____ J with his _____and chains.

ADJECTIVE   ARTICLE OF CLOTHING

In the game for _____ years, his legend remains.

NUMBER

If this rap makes you thirsty, you can _____ some Ice-T;

VERB

serve it cool, in a glass with _____ Cube for free.

NOUN

So _____ your rap history and learn it good—

VERB

from the Bronx to _____ , we run this hood!

COUNTRY

MAD LIBS® is fun to play with friends, but you can also play it by yourself! To begin with, DO NOT look at the story on the page below. Fill in the blanks on this page with the words called for. Then, using the words you have selected, fill in the blank spaces in the story.

Now you've created your own hilarious MAD LIBS® game!

COOL WHIPS

NOUN _____

NUMBER _____

ANIMAL _____

CELEBRITY _____

VEHICLE _____

NOUN _____

NOUN _____

VEHICLE _____

LETTER OF THE ALPHABET _____

NOUN _____

VERB _____

ANIMAL _____

NOUN _____

NOUN _____

ADJECTIVE _____

NOUN _____

NOUN _____

VEHICLE _____

MAD LIBS®

COOL WHIPS

Ever since I was a little _____, I've loved cars. When I was
NOUN

_____ years old, I wanted to cruise around in the
NUMBER

_____ -mobile, just like _____ . Instead,
ANIMAL   CELEBRITY

I rode in my parents' Chrysler mini-_____ with
VEHICLE

_____ -paneled doors. Now that I have my driver's
NOUN

_____ , I'm going to buy myself a red _____
NOUN   VEHICLE

like Magnum P. _____ , or maybe a luxury
LETTER OF THE ALPHABET

_____ . I plan to test- _____ a few Porsches
NOUN   VERB

and maybe a Pontiac Fire-_____ . I want my new car
ANIMAL

to be like KITT from _____ *Rider* mixed with the van
NOUN

from *The A-*_____ . My dad says I can only afford a/an
NOUN

_____ Ford Escort. My friends think I'm as dumb as a/an
ADJECTIVE

_____ for dreaming of a Camaro. But I know that one day,
NOUN

I'll be behind the _____ of the car of my dreams. Until then,
NOUN

I'll drive my grandpa's _____ , which is an awesome Yugo.
VEHICLE

MAD LIBS® is fun to play with friends, but you can also play it by yourself! To begin with, DO NOT look at the story on the page below. Fill in the blanks on this page with the words called for. Then, using the words you have selected, fill in the blank spaces in the story.

Now you've created your own hilarious MAD LIBS® game!

RIDE, SALLY RIDE

NOUN _____

ADJECTIVE _____

NUMBER _____

VERB _____

VERB _____

VERB ENDING IN "ING" _____

ADJECTIVE _____

COUNTRY _____

PLURAL NOUN _____

VERB _____

NOUN _____

PLURAL NOUN _____

PLURAL NOUN _____

NOUN _____

PLURAL NOUN _____

ADVERB _____

NOUN _____

Greetings from outer _____! My name is Sally Ride, and
                          NOUN

I'm so _____ to show you around the NASA space shuttle,
        ADJECTIVE

my home for the next _____ days. As you can _____,
                          NUMBER   VERB

we don't have much room to _____ around in here.
                                      VERB

_____ without gravity gets pretty tricky! But there's
VERB ENDING IN "ING"

plenty of room outside the shuttle, where the _____
                                                      ADJECTIVE

work happens. Yesterday, we launched two satellites for Canada and

_____. We're also conducting important science
        COUNTRY

_____. And just _____ at the amazing view out
PLURAL NOUN   VERB

the window. Earth looks like a beautiful _____ from way up
                                              NOUN

here. You can see the oceans and the _____. You can even
                                          PLURAL NOUN

see lights from big _____. It reminds you that we're all
                          PLURAL NOUN

part of one _____. I want all the little girls and little
                  NOUN

_____ around the world to dream as _____ as
PLURAL NOUN   ADVERB

they can. If you reach for the _____, you'll end up in the
                                      NOUN

stars!